THE DRUMMERS

ROGER TAYLOR

September 28, 1980: Madison Square Garden - New York City, NY

Queen drummer Roger Taylor had a unique drumming style, and his recorded 'snare' drum sound is instantly recognizable. This image taken on *The Game* tour during his drum solo at Madison Square Garden in NYC, 1980. His early main influence was Mitch Mitchell of the Jimi Hendrix Experience, also noting Keith Moon and John Bonham as influences. Roger mainly uses Ludwig drums with Zildjian and Paiste cymbals. Roger is also known to have an incredible singing voice, heard everywhere in Queen's music, background as well as taking lead vocals often.

TERRY BOZZIO

October 12, 1979: Madison Square Garden - New York City, NY

Terry Bozzio was with the English supergroup UK when I photographed him here in 1979, having just replaced Bill Bruford. Terry recorded and toured with Frank Zappa in the mid 70's appearing on the albums *Sheik Yerbouti* and *Zoot Allures* amongst others. In the 80's he formed Missing Persons with his wife Dale Bozzio. He has also been a drum clinician and has released drum instruction videos. In these images he is playing Slingerland drums with rototoms, as well as Paiste cymbals. His later drum kits have become enormous works of art literally.

October 12, 1979: Madison Square Garden - New York City, NY

IAN PAICE

October 9, 1980: Madison Square Garden - New York City, NY

A drumming legend in the hard rock world, Ian Paice was a founding member of Deep Purple and still performs with them to this day. I photographed Ian while he was with Whitesnake in 1980 at Madison Square Garden in NYC. A single bass drummer here on a Ludwig kit with Paiste cymbals, shortly after these images he switched to Pearl drums. Ian is also a left-handed drummer, he has influenced many drummers over all of these years.

October 9, 1980: Madison Square Garden - New York City, NY

July 26, 1980: Nassau Coliseum - Uniondale, New York

His drum kit has always been Ludwig, along with Paiste cymbals and Remo heads. He has also used rototoms and octobans as seen in the photos here, as well as a Paiste gong which would be lit on fire during his drum solos. His favorite drummers were Billy Cobham (here in this book), John Bonham, Keith Moon, and Ginger Baker. Alex was also known to play enormous drum kits, sometimes with *four* bass drums at times, equipped with multiple fire extinguishers for effect.

ALEX VAN HALEN

July 26, 1980: Nassau Coliseum - Uniondale, New York

Alex Van Halen, a very powerful and creative drummer to everyone that has both heard and seen him live in concert. Since 1972 when Alex and his brother Eddie along with David Lee Roth started the band, then known as Mammoth, Alex perfected his chops primarily just jamming with his brother back then on the song 'Wipe Out' by the surf rock band The Surfaris. Commonly mistaken, the term 'brown sound' was not referring to Eddie's guitar sound, but to Alex's snare drum sound.

Bobby T Torello
November 30, 1979: Madison Square Garden, New York City, NY

FOREWORD

It is with great honor that Bill asked me to write this foreword. As a young drummer, my goal in life was to play with Johnny Winter. Fast forward to November 1979, playing as a special guest for Foreigner with Johnny, at the most famous venue in the world: Madison Square Garden.

I've played for much bigger audiences 50-100,000, but the Garden, that is the ultimate venue. A sold out show to a very responsive crowd of 22,000 people. Then comes my drum solo. I abandon my drum kit to play the stage, drum sticks furiously tapping along the deck. I step up to the microphone and yell: "New York, let me see you!" 22,000 people on their feet. I couldn't hold back the tears.

What would have been an ordinary show turned into the greatest night of my career. Bill captured some of that night in photos. When I revisit these pictures, I'm flooded with the feelings of that night.

So many drummers in this book. A couple of my favorites include Ian Paice and Billy Cobham. Their performances had me wide-eyed and mouth open. I had the task of filling Tommy Aldridge's mighty big shoes in Black Oak Arkansas. Along with others, we were inducted into the Classic Drummer Hall of Fame together.

I respect every drummer in this book and could go on for days talking about them all.
Check it out for yourself, this is a read that won't disappoint.

Keep on rockin'
Bobby T Torello

Neil Peart
May 10, 1980: Palladium Theater – New York City, New York

INTRODUCTION

Thank you for viewing and reading my seventh concert photography book overall. This time I have decided to focus on *The Drummers*, 34 of them in fact. Any concert photographer will tell you that getting a great shot of a drummer in action is not easy at all, it can be very difficult depending on your angle of view, as well as the drummer's drum set and where he sits within that drum kit. I've been in shooting positions where you could not even see the drummer at all, unfortunately Cozy Powell with the Michael Schenker Group in 1980 for example.

Anyway, I have included my best images of a variety of drummers here and I hope you enjoy viewing them. I would also like to make a disclaimer, I am a photographer first and foremost, my writings and descriptions are purely observational and NOT technical to the drum equipment world, if I've made a mistake in labeling a drum kit wrong, I sincerely apologize to the drum purists.

Enjoy,
Bill O'Leary
Timeless Concert Images

p.s. For personally signed 8"x10" full color prints, please contact me directly via timelessconcertimages@gmail.com. Also, check out timelessconcertimages.com.

Andy Parker
Mikkey Dee
Cliff Davies
Alan Gratzer
Bruce Crump
Bobby T Torello
Tommy Aldridge
Dave Lombardo
Bobby Rondinelli
Monte Yoho
Chris Layton
Tony Brock
Alan White
Dennis Elliott
Lee Kundrat
Stewart Copeland
Neil Peart

Alex Van Halen
Ian Paice
Terry Bozzio
Roger Taylor
Eric Carr
Billy Cobham
Simon Phillips
Charlie Benante
Phil Taylor
Frank Beard
Mick Fleetwood
Gil Moore
Mark Craney
Jon Fishman
Jeff Sipe
Rod Morgenstein
John Panozzo

Photographs and text by Bill O'Leary
Printed and distributed by Bill O'Leary
Published by Bill O'Leary
Front and back cover designs by Mary Prato
Formatting and interior design by Greg Prato
Front Cover Photo: Rod Morgenstein
Back Cover Photo: Neil Peart
Professional drum consulting by Tim Elliott

ISBN: 9798386885861

THE DRUMMERS

Words and Photography
By Bill O'Leary

Foreword By
Bobby T Torello

ERIC CARR

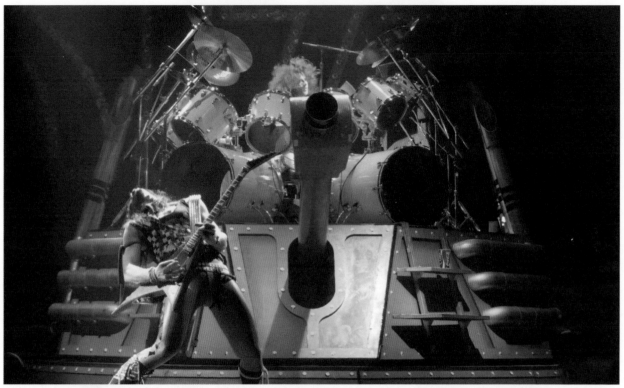

January 25, 1984: Denver University Arena - Denver, Colorado

A beloved drummer, Eric Carr replaced Peter Criss in Kiss back in 1980. I photographed Eric here on the *Lick It Up* tour in 1984 with his huge drum kit perched upon a tank turret onstage. He recorded and toured on seven Kiss albums to my count. He has mentioned his influences as John Bonham, Lenny White, and Keith Moon. He played Ludwig drums with Paiste and RUDE cymbals. Eric tragically passed away at the age of 41 in 1991.

November 1, 1980: Capitol Theatre - Passaic, New Jersey

BILLY COBHAM

November 1, 1980: Capitol Theatre - Passaic, New Jersey

'Legend' does not even begin to describe Billy Cobham, I photographed Billy here with Bobby and the Midnites in 1980, Bob Weir's side project. He is known as 'the' jazz-fusion pioneer, previously having worked with Miles Davis, Mahavishnu Orchestra, and Tommy Bolin on Billy's own classic solo album, 'Spectrum,' in 1973. One of the most powerful drummers I had ever seen play, and his list of recordings is endless. Billy played Tama drums and Sabian cymbals. Legend and beyond.

SIMON PHILLIPS

October 7, 1980: Capitol Theatre - Passaic, New Jersey

One of the most incredible session drummers of all time, Simon Phillips photographed here in 1980 on the *There & Back* Tour with Jeff Beck. I personally first became aware of Simon's drumming on the Judas Priest album *Sin After Sin* in 1977, followed by one of my favorite albums, *Back on the Streets* by Gary Moore in 1978, and then early 1980 on the self-titled debut by the Michael Schenker Group.

October 7, 1980: Capitol Theatre - Passaic, New Jersey

Photographed here on this night behind his very impressive Tama drum kit. He was truly mesmerizing to watch perform, especially his double bass drum technique which he has been credited with, hugely influencing many metal drummers later. Simon would go on to work on hundreds of studio recordings as well as a long-term gig with the band Toto, replacing another amazing drummer, Jeff Porcaro.

June 26, 1987: Normans Place - Aurora, Colorado

CHARLIE BENANTE

June 26, 1987: Normans Place - Aurora, Colorado

I photographed Charlie here from behind the drum kit with his permission, Anthrax were touring in support of their album *Among the Living* in 1987. Considered one of the best drummers in the thrash metal genre, Charlie is also known to be a pioneer in the double-bass speed and blast beat technique. Endorsed by Tama drums as well as Paiste cymbals, along with Vic Firth sticks. An incredible drummer, case in point, the Stormtroopers of Death album, *Speak English or Die*, one of my personal favorites.

May 2, 1981: Palladium Theater - New York City, NY

PHIL TAYLOR

May 2, 1981: Palladium Theater - New York City, NY

Original Motörhead drummer Phil Taylor photographed here on their *Ace of Spades* Tour in 1981. Phil was a beast of a drummer who is often credited with the 'speed' or 'blast' double bass technique, as was first heard on the title track of Motörhead's *Overkill* album in 1979. In an early interview, he compared his double bass technique to running very fast. His drum set here is a Camco kit with a mirror finish and 'spade' front skin covers for the *Ace of Spades* Tour.

FRANK BEARD

May 4, 1980: Capitol Theatre - Passaic, New Jersey

ZZ Top drummer Frank Beard has been the backbone of ZZ Top's music from the very beginning. Before that, he was a member of The Moving Sidewalks briefly with Billy Gibbons in May of 1969, and he introduced Dusty Hill to Gibbons as well, which led to the formation of the band later that same year. Frank's nickname early on was 'Rube' or 'Rube Beard.' And despite his name, was the only member of ZZ Top without a beard!

May 4, 1980: Capitol Theatre - Passaic, New Jersey

I photographed Frank and ZZ Top here on the *Deguello* Tour in 1980, at The Capitol Theatre in Passaic, New Jersey. Frank has used Tama drums and Paiste cymbals, along with Promark sticks. The list of radio hits Frank has played on is too long to list here. Known as a rock steady drummer keeping time with the best of them in the style of Charlie Watts and Phil Rudd. For 51 years and some 15 studio albums, Frank Beard was behind the drum kit for "That Lil' Old Band from Texas."

August 7, 1992: Fox Theatre - Boulder, Colorado

MICK FLEETWOOD

August 7, 1992: Fox Theatre - Boulder, Colorado

Mick Fleetwood was photographed her in 1992 on his DW drum kit while on tour with his side project, Mick Fleetwood's The Zoo. Mick is a living legend, having had his start in 1963 in London. By early 1967, he had joined John Mayall & the Bluesbreakers, followed by the newly-formed Fleetwood Mac later that year. In the mid 70's, he achieved massive success with the addition of Lindsey Buckingham and Stevie Nicks to Fleetwood Mac. While photographing him here in 1992, I noticed he was a very charismatic drummer with an awesome swing to his style.

GIL MOORE

June 21, 1980: Capitol Theatre - Passaic, New Jersey

Founding member of the Canadian band Triumph, Gil Moore is one of the few
drummers that also takes on the lead vocalist role (splitting vocal duties with guitarist
Rik Emmett in the band). I photographed Triumph and Gil here in 1980 on their
Progressions of Power tour. An incredible drummer, Gil played a Tama Imperialstar
Saturn kit with a platinum finish, as well as Sabian cymbals early on, then Zildjian.
For the past 30 years, Gil has owned Metalworks Studios in Ontario, Canada's largest
recording facility.

MARK CRANEY

October 9, 1980: Madison Square Garden - New York City, NY

Mark was another amazing drummer who passed away early (at the age of 53). I photographed him here in 1980 with Jethro Tull at Madison Square Garden in NYC. His list of credits is impressive, Tommy Bolin tour in 1976, Gino Vannelli in 1978, Jean Luc Ponty tour in 1976 as well. Mark played a Ludwig Mahogany or possibly Cherry kit here in this picture, but also played Sonor and Gretsch kits. Every drummer that has spoken of Mark has said that he was one of the best.

JON FISHMAN

April 5, 1992: Fox Theatre - Boulder, Colorado

Jon Fishman is the co-founding drummer of the band Phish. He is known for wearing a 'muumuu' when performing behind the kit. An eclectic guy with a drum kit that consists of almost every brand name from the percussion world, including Gretsch, Yamaha, Ludwig, Zildjian, Sabian, Paiste and Istanbul Agop cymbal (seen in the above photo). His most unique percussive tool is a 1965 Blue Electrolux vacuum cleaner that he has 'played' since 1989.

JEFF SIPE

November 14, 1992: Fox Theatre - Boulder, Colorado

Jeff Sipe is a founding member of Aquarium Rescue Unit, photographed here at one of their shows back in 1992. One of the most creative and accomplished drummers, he attended Berklee School of Music, played with Jonas Hellborg and Shawn Lane, Leftover Salmon, and his own experimental band, Zambiland Orchestra to name a handful. Jeff is quoted as saying, "Drumming is about surrender and submission." Jeff plays Sonor Drums and Zildjian cymbals. He is a drum teacher and clinician, as well.

ROD MORGENSTEIN

June 16, 1992: Fox Theatre - Boulder, Colorado

I first heard Rod Morgenstein on the Dixie Dregs album *Free Fall* back in 1977. I was immediately floored by the drumming, particularly his flair and his cymbal work. Rod can play any style of music with ease from jazz fusion with the Dixie Dregs to rock with the band Winger. He has also held down a position at the Berklee College of Music as a professor for over 20 years as a music educator.

June 16, 1992: Fox Theatre - Boulder, Colorado

I photographed Rod here with the Dixie Dregs (aka The Dregs) on their *Bring 'Em Back Alive* reunion tour in 1992 on multiple nights. Sitting behind his Premier drum kit with Sabian Cymbals surrounding him, the always-smiling drummer was a joy to watch. No one makes playing the drums look more fun than Rod. He is currently working on his 50th year of playing drums as this book is published.

JOHN PANOZZO

February 6, 1980: Madison Square Garden - New York City, NY

John was a founding member of Styx and played with them up until 1984, at the end of the *Kilroy Was Here* tour. I photographed him here at Madison Square Garden in NYC in 1980 on their *Cornerstone* tour. I loved the look of John's drum kit complete with 'gong,' and not one, but two 'cowbells' (a 70's essential).

February 6, 1980: Madison Square Garden - New York City, NY

John played a Tama kit with Zildjian cymbals, surrounded by various percussion pieces as seen in these images. On this night I was mesmerized by his playing, he was very powerful yet played with great precision and skill. Sadly, John passed away at the young age of 47 years old, just 16 years after these images above.

ANDY PARKER

February 29, 1980: Capitol Theatre - Passaic, New Jersey

A founding member of the band UFO, Andy Parker has been drumming for 55 years or so. I photographed Andy here in early 1980 on their *No Place to Run* tour. Andy helped form the band back in 1968, they gained popularity when German guitarist Michael Schenker joined in 1973, and continued with what many called the greatest live album of the 70's, *Strangers in the Night*.

February 29, 1980: Capitol Theatre - Passaic, New Jersey

Andy Parker played a Ludwig Vistalite kit with Paiste cymbals as seen here in these images from 1980. His favorite drummer was John Bonham, but was influenced by Keith Moon, Ginger Baker, and Mitch Mitchell as well. A very powerful rock drummer, Andy has played on some of the most iconic UFO songs, 'Lights Out,' 'Rock Bottom,' and 'Pack It Up (And Go).'

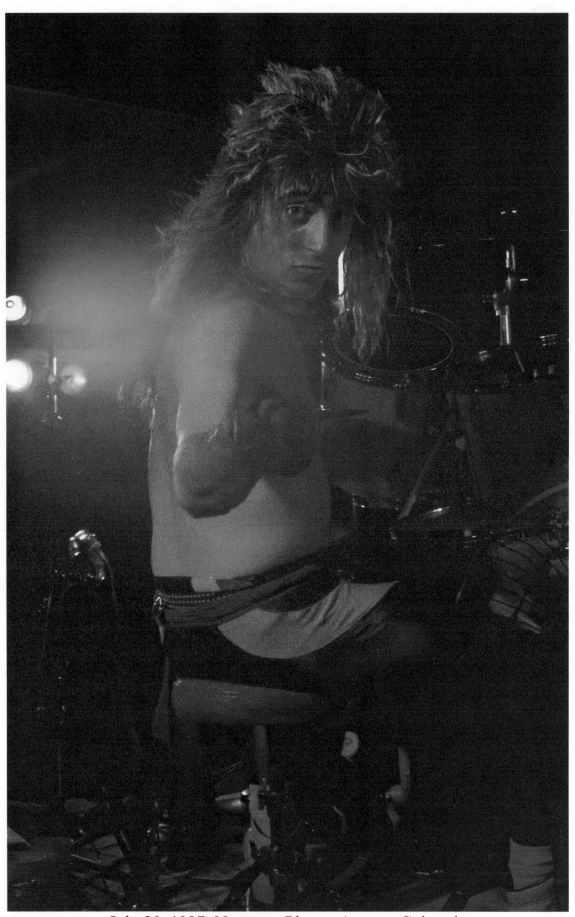

July 30, 1987: Normans Place - Aurora, Colorado

MIKKEY DEE

July 30, 1987: Normans Place - Aurora, Colorado

Swedish drummer Mikkey Dee photographed here in 1987 while on tour with King Diamond early in his career. Later joining Motörhead for 23 years, then becoming a full-time member of the Scorpions in 2016. Playing Sonor drums and Paiste cymbals with Remo heads, Mikkey, it's safe to say, has rocked the world as a drummer. He was and is a very animated and entertaining drummer, not to mention his technical abilities of course, one of the best, every band he has played with were lucky to have him, very friendly and approachable too.

CLIFF DAVIES

July 14, 1980: Spectrum Arena - Philadelphia, Pennsylvania

British drummer Cliff Davies was the original drummer in Ted Nugent's band after leaving the Amboy Dukes to go solo in 1975. Cliff was also a skilled engineer and producer in the studio, and co-produced much of those early albums, uncredited. He is photographed here in 1980 on the *Scream Dream* tour, his last with Ted Nugent, on a simple Ludwig drum kit with Zildjian cymbals. Sadly, Cliff took his life by his own hand in April 2008 at his home in Atlanta.

ALAN GRATZER

September 13, 1980: Madison Square Garden - New York City, NY

A founding member of REO Speedwagon, Alan Gratzer has been hitting the skins since 1966, playing on some 12 studio albums, including their chart topping *Hi Infidelity* album and tour in 1980/1981. He retired from touring with the band in 1988, then would do occasional guest appearances after that. Alan played Ludwig drums. Known as an amazingly solid rock drummer, Alan also provided background vocals from behind his kit.

BRUCE CRUMP

November 29, 1979: Madison Square Garden - New York City, NY

Molly Hatchet drummer Bruce Crump played on the band's biggest hits, *Flirtin' with Disaster, Gator Country,* and *Beatin' the Odds* just to name a few. I photographed Bruce here on the *Flirtin' with Disaster* tour at Madison Square Garden in NYC at one of the bands biggest shows of their career. A solid and powerful drummer, who later spent time teaching drums when not playing in Molly Hatchet. Sadly, Bruce passed at 57 years old of throat cancer in 2015.

BOBBY T TORELLO

November 30, 1979: Madison Square Garden - New York City, NY

I photographed Bobby T Torello here with Johnny Winter while playing Madison Square Garden in NYC, back in 1979 on the *White Hot & Blue* tour. Before that, he had replaced Tommy Aldridge in Black Oak Arkansas, and later worked with Michael Bolton and Grace Slick. An incredible ball of energy drummer who plays with a relentless style. A member of the Classic Drummer Hall of Fame.

TOMMY ALDRIDGE

April 19, 1980: Palladium Theater - New York City, NY

One of the best rock drummers of the last 50 years and counting, Tommy Aldridge first started with Black Oak Arkansas back in 1972. He is another pioneer of the double bass drum sound in rock drumming, and is also known for his bare-handed drumming during his drum solo spots live. A favorite live album of mine, *Raunch 'N' Roll Live* by Black Oak Arkansas features an early Aldridge drum solo.

March 12, 1984: McNichols Arena - Denver, Colorado

Tommy is photographed here two different times, once in 1980 with the Pat Travers Band and in 1984 with Ozzy Osbourne. Since 1980 Tommy has been playing Yamaha drums with various cymbals, including Zildjian, and Paiste, who he currently endorses. One of the best drummers I've seen, who never seems to age! He has toured and recorded the last 10+ years with Whitesnake. I saw him in 2018 at 68 years old playing like he was in his 20's.

DAVE LOMBARDO

January 18, 1991: Mammoth Events Center - Denver, Colorado

Co-founding member of the thrash metal band Slayer, Dave is widely known as one of the very best drummers of the genre. Photographed here with Slayer on the *Seasons in the Abyss* tour. Another pioneer of the double bass style, who is known for his aggressive style and attack. Dave has played Tama kits with Paiste cymbals for many years. Having seen Dave play live many, many times, I would describe his playing as technically precise and relentless. Amazing. He has continued his career playing for many bands including Suicidal Tendencies, Mr. Bungle, and as of most recently, Testament.

BOBBY RONDINELLI

May 8, 1981: Capitol Theatre - Passaic, New Jersey

I photographed Bobby Rondinelli early in his career, here with Rainbow in 1981, and seen here playing a Sonor kit with Paiste cymbals. He has moved on to Ludwig drums with Attack drumheads, as well as continuing with Paiste. He has since played with many bands, including Black Sabbath, Blue Öyster Cult, Axel Rudi Pell, and Quiet Riot to name a few. He also continues his career with a very busy schedule teaching, as well as holding drum clinics.

MONTE YOHO

November 29, 1979: Madison Square Garden - New York City, NY

Monte Yoho was with the Outlaws from the very beginning (back in 1972), when they were formed by guitarist Hughie Thomasson. He co-wrote some of their biggest hits, including 'The Goes Another Love Song' and 'Green Grass and High Tides.' Photographed here in 1979, Monte is playing a Gretsch kit and Paiste cymbals. One of Monte's biggest influences was Russ Kunkel and many of the early country rock drummers of the early 70's. In later years, Monte switched to Beier drums.

CHRIS LAYTON

April 14, 1992: Fox Theatre - Boulder, Colorado

Chris Layton (who is mainly known as a founding member of Stevie Ray Vaughan's Double Trouble) is photographed here in 1992, with his later band, Arc Angels. Playing a Tama kit with Sabian cymbals in these image, he was also known to play a Ludwig kit with Zildjian cymbals, as well. Chris has since been playing drums for Kenny Wayne Shepherd and Buddy Guy.

February 6, 1980: Madison Square Garden - New York City, NY

TONY BROCK

February 6, 1980: Madison Square Garden - New York City, NY

British-born drummer Tony Brock has been with The Babys since their formation in the mid 70's. He is photographed here in early 1980 on their *Union Jacks* tour at Madison Square Garden in NYC. After The Babys, Tony joined Rod Stewart's band for 12 years, as well as Jimmy Barnes' band in Australia. Tony spends time now playing in a reformed version of The Babys, and also running his recording studio, Silver Dreams Studios. Tony plays both Ludwig and DW drums with Remo heads and Zildjian cymbals.

ALAN WHITE

September 6, 1980: Madison Square Garden - New York City, NY

Legendary drummer Alan White played with Yes for most of his career, beginning in 1972 when he replaced drummer Bill Bruford. Previous to this, he worked with John Lennon on his *Imagine* album in 1971, drumming on iconic songs 'Instant Karma' and the title track. The 1973 Yes album, *Tales from Topographic Oceans*, was the first to feature Alan.

September 6, 1980: Madison Square Garden - New York City, NY

I photographed Alan here in 1980 on Yes' *Drama* tour at Madison Square Garden, NYC, where the band played 'in the round' (a rotating round stage which enabled these unique photo angles). Classic Yes albums *Relayer* and *Going for the One* feature some of Alan's great playing. Alan played a Ludwig Drum kit and Zildjian cymbals. Sadly, Alan passed in 2022, at the age of 72.

November 30, 1979: Madison Square Garden - New York City, NY

DENNIS ELLIOTT

November 30, 1979: Madison Square Garden - New York City, NY

British drummer Dennis Elliott is best known as the drummer and 'pulse' of Foreigner for 16 years, starting in 1976. An incredibly talented drummer who has played on some of the biggest radio hits ever, I photographed Dennis here in 1979 at Madison Square Garden in NYC, on Foreigner's *Head Games* tour. I believe Dennis was playing a Ludwig kit in these photos here.

November 12, 1986: DJ's Rock Club - Colorado Springs, Colorado

LEE KUNDRAT

June 9, 1987: Normans Place - Aurora, Colorado

Rat Skates was a founding member of the band Overkill in the early 80's. His very early drumming influence was Peter Criss of Kiss, then quickly followed by Les Binks of Judas Priest, Clive Burr of Iron Maiden, and Phil Taylor of Motörhead. Rat played a Ludwig kit with Zildjian cymbals primarily. These images were taken on both the 1986 *Feel the Fire* tour and 1987 *Taking Over* tour. After leaving Overkill in 1987, Rat began a career as a drumming instructor, and performed many drum clinics as well.

January 10, 1981: Madison Square Garden - New York City, NY

STEWART COPELAND

January 10, 1981: Madison Square Garden - New York City, NY

Stewart Copeland of The Police (photographed here in 1981) is known as one of the most influential drummers of his time. He was also known to have had an influence upon the great drummer Neil Peart of Rush. A true innovator, his is seen here behind his Tama kit, where you can also see the 'octobans' which he helped develop with Tama, as well as a 'splash cymbal' he helped develop with Paiste. He was also a left-handed drummer playing on a right-handed drum kit. Stewart would later become a composer of motion picture soundtracks, with great success.

May 10, 1980: Palladium Theater - New York City, NY

NEIL PEART

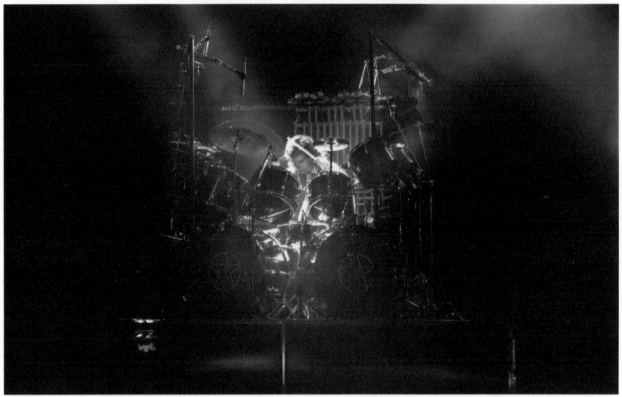

May 10, 1980: Palladium Theater - New York City, NY

Where do I start? 'Pratt' was an early nickname given to Neil by his bandmates Geddy Lee and Alex Lifeson. Neil joined Rush in 1974, replacing original drummer John Rutsey, and they soon recorded the band's second album, *Fly By Night* (finding out beforehand that Neil was quite the lyricist, as well as an amazing drummer). Any drummer will tell you, that one of the greatest drumming albums of all time is their album *2112*, that features an incredible display of technique and finesse.

May 11, 1980: Palladium Theater - New York City, NY

May 10, 1980: Palladium Theater - New York City, NY

I photographed Neil (by this time widely known as 'The Professor') with Rush eight different times, starting with the *Hemispheres* tour. The six images here are all from their four-night run in May 1980 at the Palladium Theater in NYC. This was their tour for their breakthrough album, *Permanent Waves*. This tour's images I consider my best of Neil. On this tour, he was playing a beautiful Tama Rosewood kit with Zildjian cymbals, with an array of percussion that surrounded his drum kit.

May 11, 1980: Palladium Theater - New York City, NY

May 11, 1980: Palladium Theater - New York City, NY

Certainly one of my personal favorite drummers of all-time, Neil has said that he was initially influenced by Keith Moon, Ginger Baker, and John Bonham growing up, and soon after, he discovered the talents of Buddy Rich and Gene Krupa. I must add here that Neil was also an amazing author, publishing books on his travels and tragedies he faced in his life. Neil retired from touring with Rush in 2015, and sadly, Neil passed away at his home in California on January 7, 2020. Rest in peace, Neil.